SOCCER

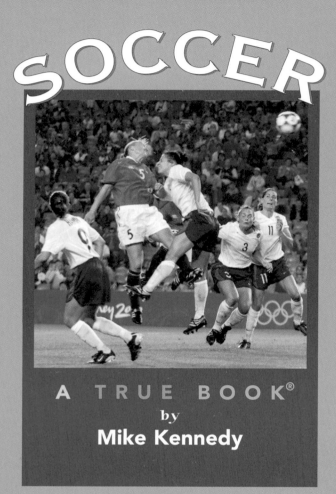

A TRUE BOOK®

by

Mike Kennedy

Children's Press®
A Division of Scholastic Inc.

New York Toronto London Auckland Sydney
Mexico City New Delhi Hong Kong
Danbury, Connecticut

A goalkeeper diving
to make a save

Reading Consultant
Nanci R. Vargus, *Ed.D.*
Teacher in Residence
University of Indianapolis
Indianapolis, Indiana

Library of Congress Cataloging-in-Publication Data

Kennedy, Mike (Mike William), 1965-
    Soccer / by Mike Kennedy.
        p. cm. — (A true book)
    Summary: Presents the history, rules, equipment, and positions of
soccer, as well as a list of some of the best players of all time.
    Includes bibliographical references (p.   ) and index.
    ISBN 0-516-22337-2 (lib. bdg.)   0-516-29374-5 (pbk.)
    1. Soccer—Juvenile literature. [1. Soccer.] I. Title. II. Series.
GV943.25 .K47 2002
796.334—dc21   2002005285

CHILDREN'S PRESS, AND A TRUE BOOK®, and associated logos are
trademarks and or registered trademarks of Grolier Publishing Co., Inc.
SCHOLASTIC and associated logos are trademarks and or registered
trademarks of Scholastic Inc.

1 2 3 4 5 6 7 8 9 10 R 11 10 09 08 07 06 05 04 03 02

Contents

Soccer is enjoyed by players of all ages.

The Simplest Game

An old saying goes "Rome wasn't built in a day." In other words, it took a very long time for this ancient **empire** to rise to power. You could say almost the same thing about soccer. The sport was "born" in the Far East about 2,000 years ago when Chinese soldiers participated in

A team about to play *kemari*, an ancient Japanese kicking game similar to soccer

a kicking game known as *tsu-shu*. Some 600 years later, a similar sport called *kemari* developed in Japan.

The ancient Greeks and Romans were next to discover

soccer. The Romans enjoyed a very rough version called *harpastum*. The object was to advance a ball across the opponent's end line—by any means necessary. Roman soldiers introduced *harpastum* to people in other lands. Europeans, especially citizens of the country now known as England, loved the sport. By the 1300s, the English had renamed *harpastum* "football." It remained, however, a violent game.

By the 1860s, the term "soccer" was being used as often as "football" to describe the sport. (Today, the game is called "soccer" in the United States and Canada and "football" everywhere else in the world. American football is an entirely different sport).

It was also at this time that soccer really became the game you know today. That is when England's Football Association adopted a set of rules known as "The Simplest Game." The most

Schoolchildren playing an early version of soccer in the mid-1800s

important rule limited the use of hands. Kicking became the sport's most useful skill.

In the decades that followed, soccer's popularity grew tremendously. It became an

Olympic sport in 1908. The first World Cup tournament was held 22 years later. Professional leagues then began to sprout up all over Europe. Players from different nations shared secrets with each other, and the game continued to improve.

In the 1970s, many top players came to the United States to join the North American Soccer League (NASL). The NASL helped Americans get excited about soccer. Today, the United States, like all other

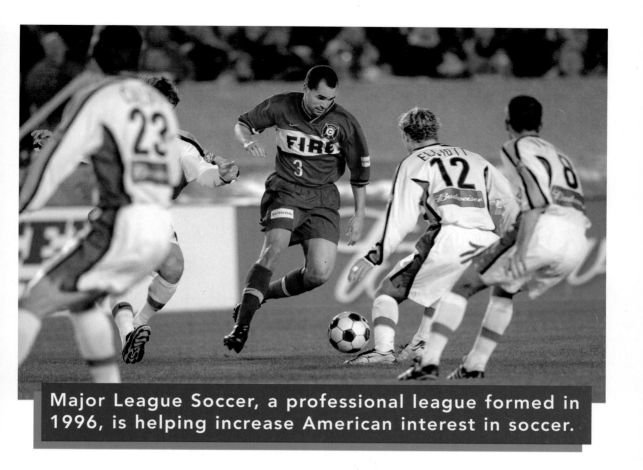

Major League Soccer, a professional league formed in 1996, is helping increase American interest in soccer.

nations, has professional leagues, as well as men's and women's teams that compete in tournaments worldwide.

Here's the Pitch

Doesn't "here's the pitch" sound like something said during a baseball game? A pitch, however, is also a term that is used to describe a soccer field.

A pitch is very large. It can run as long as 130 yards (119 meters) and as wide as 100 yards (91 m). The white lines running

A soccer field is called a "pitch."

the length of the field are called sidelines. Those running the width at each end are known as goal lines. The midfield line splits the field in two equal halves.

Directly in the center of the field is a circle. The ball is placed here

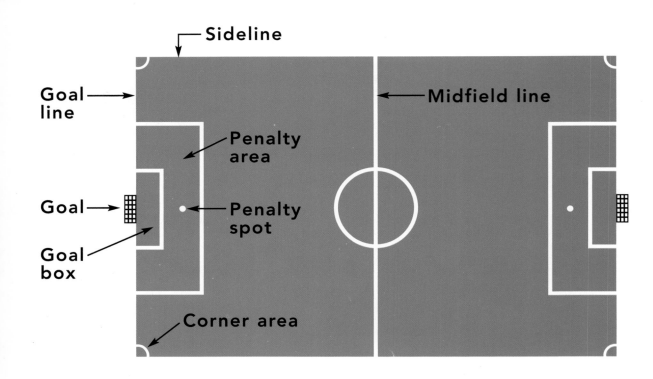

Sideline

Midfield line

Goal line

Penalty area

Goal

Penalty spot

Goal box

Corner area

for kickoffs at the start of each half, and after a goal is scored.

The goals are located at each end of the field. Each stands 8 feet (2.4 m) tall and 24 feet (7 m) wide. The small rectangle in front of the goal is called the goal box. Goalkeepers cannot be kicked, bumped, or shoved when they are in this space. The larger rectangle in front of the goal is known as the penalty area. It includes a white spot where the ball is placed for **penalty kicks**.

A player trying to score on a penalty kick

Hands Off

The object of soccer is to score more goals than your opponent. But you can't use your hands to send the ball past the goalkeeper. You may advance the ball only with your feet, shins, knees, thighs, hips, midsection, and head. Your opponent gets a **free kick** if you break this rule.

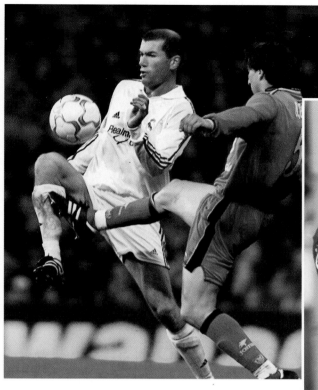

In soccer, it's legal to advance the ball with your knees (above left), chest (above right), or even your head (left).

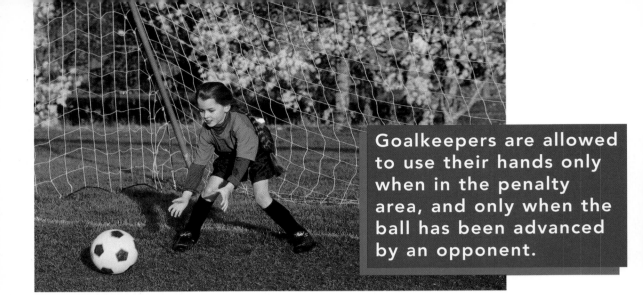

Goalkeepers are allowed to use their hands only when in the penalty area, and only when the ball has been advanced by an opponent.

The "no hands" rule is a little different for goalkeepers. They are allowed to use their hands to block a shot or pick up a ball kicked by an opponent—as long as they are in the penalty area.

Soccer matches are divided into two halves. Each begins

with a kickoff, where one team is given possession of the ball to begin an offensive attack. Once a match starts, the clock does not stop running—except at halftime. If a player is hurt, play is halted. "Injury time" is then added at the end of the half.

After the kickoff, anyone can take control of the ball.

If your team knocks the ball across a sideline, your opponent gets to put the ball back in play with a "throw-in." With both hands on the ball, the player launches the ball from behind his or her head. The player is allowed to get a running start, but both feet must be on the ground and behind the sideline when the ball is released.

If the ball crosses the goal line and the attacking team touched it last, a goal kick (a free kick from the goal area) is

Players putting the ball back in play with a corner kick (left) and a throw-in (right)

awarded to the defending team. If the ball crosses the goal line and the defending team touched it last, the attacking team gets a corner kick—a free kick from the corner area closest to where the ball went out of bounds. The corner areas are the white semi-circles in each corner of the field.

You can run anywhere on the field during a game as long as you do not go offside. This means you cannot receive a pass if you have run ahead of the defense and are standing alone with only the goalkeeper left to stop you.

The referee and linesmen enforce the rules during a game. They stop the action whenever they spot an **infraction**. That includes when someone is playing too rough.

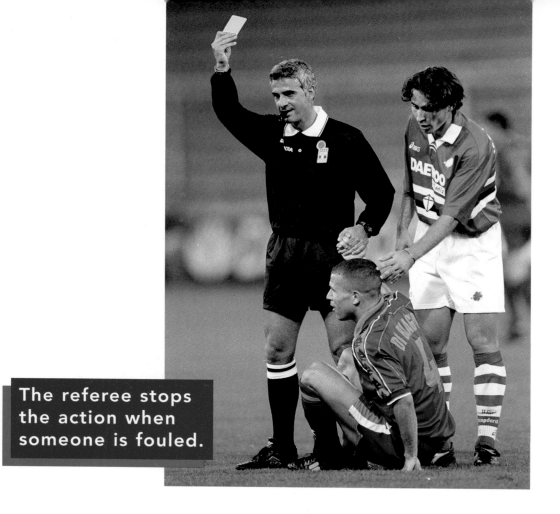

The referee stops the action when someone is fouled.

The referee, in fact, can order a player to leave the field if that player has put others in danger.

The Positions

Eleven players take the field for each team in a soccer match. Each plays one of four basic positions: forward, defender, midfielder, or goalkeeper. All have offensive and defensive responsibilities. That is because teams are constantly shifting from offense to defense during a game.

Since there are constant battles for the ball in soccer, everyone on the field is responsible for playing offense and defense.

Use the inside of your foot to help control the ball (above). Only experienced players should try to "head" the ball (right).

Forwards are also known as strikers or attackers. Some forwards are positioned near the sidelines to set up teammates in front of the goal. They must be able to "dribble" well. In soccer, dribbling is controlling the ball with your feet as you move downfield.

Forwards must also be able to "cross" the ball accurately. A cross is a pass that travels from either sideline toward the goal.

Forwards stationed in the middle of the field try to turn scoring chances into goals. They usually have quick moves, can jump high, and shoot the ball hard.

Who prevents forwards from scoring? Defenders, also called fullbacks. They normally do not stray too far from their end of the field. Their main responsibility is to guard, or "mark," opponents and clear the ball from in front of the net. Defenders also must start the

A defender (at left) attempting to block a shot

A midfielder goes to the ground trying to stop a forward from advancing the ball.

offense by scanning the field and passing the ball to a midfielder.

Midfielders, or halfbacks, roam between the defenders and forwards. On defense, they help out until their team regains control of the ball. On offense, they look for forwards in scoring position and try to hit them with **pinpoint** passes. Aggressive midfielders will race toward the goal if they think they can score.

A goalkeeper often rises high in the air to block a pass or shot.

The goalkeeper's job is to stop the ball from going in the net. **Anticipation** is key.

Strong hands, long arms, and good jumping ability also help. So does a loud voice to shout instructions to your teammates.

Coaches can use any combination of players they choose. Of course, the goalkeeper always stays on the field to protect the goal. Sometimes, a coach sends in substitutes. For example, if your team has the lead, your coach may put in an extra defender and take out an attacker.

Going Global

Which country has the best men's soccer team? What about the best women's team? Those questions are answered once every four years during a tournament called the World Cup.

The World Cup is sponsored by the Federation Internationale de Football Association (FIFA).

During the World Cup,
players do whatever it
takes to win.

FIFA is an international organization dedicated to soccer. It
staged its first tournament in

Italy's and Hungary's team captains shake hands before the start of the 1938 World Cup final in Paris.

1930 in Uruguay. Only twelve countries made the long and tiring trip, and the Uruguayans took the title on their home soil.

Italy captured the next two World Cups before play was suspended because of World War II. When the tournament resumed in 1950, the number of countries that competed in it increased. That drew even more fans to the event. Winning the World Cup was now a matter of national pride.

The World Cup soon became a launching pad for soccer's most spectacular stars. The brightest of them was a

Brazilian soccer star Pelé (far right) raises his hands in celebration after scoring the winning goal in the 1958 World Cup final.

Brazilian nicknamed Pelé. He burst onto the scene in 1958. That year, as a 17-year-old, he led Brazil to its first championship with **breathtaking** play.

By 1966, the World Cup was being televised worldwide. A different player took center stage every tournament. There was Eusebio of Portugal, Franz Beckenbauer of West Germany,

Eusebio in action during the 1966 World Cup final between Portugal and Hungary

and Diego Maradona of Argentina, just to name a few.

Thanks in part to the World Cup, the sport of soccer took off. Before long, women wanted the thrill of competing for their countries. FIFA granted their wish in 1991 with the Women's World Cup. The United States claimed the first title. Eight years later, the Americans did it again in a thrilling battle against China. The match confirmed the

Joy Fawcett was one of the stars for the United States in the 1999 Women's World Cup final against China.

World Cup—both the men's and women's—as the world's most popular sporting event.

Soccer Stars

Here are ten of soccer's greatest players:

Stanley Matthews (England, forward, 1932-1965)
The "Wizard of Dribble" set the standard for all English players who followed him.

Stanley Matthews

Lev Yashin (Russia, goalkeeper, 1951-1970)
Nothing got by the "Black Octopus," who always wore a dark shirt and had long arms that went "everywhere."

Lev Yashin

Pelé (Brazil, forward, 1958-1977)
His real name is Edson Arantes do Nascimento, and he was simply the best soccer player ever.

Pelé

Alfredo Di Stefano (Argentina, forward, 1942-1965)
Always in the right place at the right time, Di Stefano defined the term "all-around player."

Alfredo Di Stefano

Eusebio

Eusebio (Portugal, forward, 1961-1979)
The "Black Panther" was a deadly goal scorer and probably Pelé's fiercest rival.

Johan Cruyff (the Netherlands, forward, 1964-1984)
Cruyff revolutionized the sport by creating an exciting style of play known as "Total Soccer."

Johan Cruyff

Franz Beckenbauer (West Germany, sweeper, 1962-1983)
No one understood the game better than the "Kaiser," who literally invented his position of sweeper.

Franz Beckenbauer

Diego Maradona (Argentina, forward, 1976-1997)
Perhaps the fastest player ever, Maradona dominated soccer for more than a decade.

Diego Maradona

Michelle Akers (United States, forward, 1985-2000)
Nothing slowed her down, not even a disease called chronic fatigue syndrome.

Michelle Akers

Mia Hamm (United States, forward, 1989-present)
Voted U.S. Soccer Player of the Year more times than anyone, she holds the international goal-scoring record.

Mia Hamm

To Find Out More

Here are some additional resources to help you learn more about soccer:

 **Books**

Rutledge, Rachel. **Women of Sports: The Best of the Best in Soccer.** The Millbrook Press, 1998.

Stewart, Mark. **Soccer: A History of the World's Most Popular Game.** Franklin Watts, 1998.

Organizations and Online Sites

**American Youth
Soccer Organization**
http://www.soccer.org

Official site of one of the largest youth organizations in the United States. Includes a soccer primer as well as information on tournaments and membership.

**Canadian Soccer
Association**
http://www.canadasoccer.com

Includes late-breaking news as well as information on Canada's national team and youth leagues.

FIFA
http://www.fifa.com

Includes the latest on the World Cup as well as information on all other programs and events sponsored by FIFA.

Major League Soccer
http://www.mlsnet.com

Official site of Major League Soccer.

**United States
Soccer Federation**
http://www.us-soccer.com

Includes information on men's and women's national teams.

**United States Youth
Soccer Association**
http://usysa.org

Includes playing tips, news on regional and national tournaments, and advice for parents and coaches.

Women's Soccer World
http://www.womensoccer.com

Devoted to covering women's soccer around the globe.

**Women's United
Soccer Association**
http://www.wusaleague.com

Official site of the Women's United Soccer Association.

Important Words

anticipation expecting something to happen before it does

breathtaking amazing

dominate to rule over, to be the greatest one at something

empire when one country rules over many others

free kick kick awarded to one team when a member of the other team touches the ball with a hand or commits a foul

infraction violation, breaking of the rules

penalty kick a free kick directly at the goal taken inside the penalty box

pinpoint to carefully aim at

revolutionized changed in a major way

Index

Meet the Author

Mike Kennedy is a freelance sportswriter whose work has ranged from Super Bowl coverage to historical research and analysis. He has profiled athletes in virtually every sport, including Peyton Manning, Bernie Williams, and Allen Iverson. He is a graduate of Franklin & Marshall College in Lancaster, Pennsylvania.

Mike has contributed his expertise to other books for young people, such as *Auto Racing: A History of Fast Cars and Fearless Drivers.* He has authored four other sports True Books, including *Basketball* and *Football.*